# Ordinary but Extraordinary

## The Sammy and Bertha McNally Story

Christine Bell with
Victor Maxwell

All proceeds from this book go to the ministry of
Pastor G. S. Nair, People's Baptist Ministries, Kerala, India

To Bertha,
my admiration and affection.
To my husband David and my children,
Esther, Joshua and Caleb, thank you
for all your love, support and
encouragement.

Foreword ................................................. 3

Chapter 1    The Livingstons ................................ 5

Chapter 2    Family Business or
             the Father's Business ........................ 9

Chapter 3    India ....................................... 13

Chapter 4    Curtains and Looms .......................... 20

Chapter 5    Out of the Blue ............................. 24

Chapter 6    A New Beginning ............................. 30

Chapter 7    Seaview ..................................... 36

Chapter 8    Moving In and Moving On ..................... 41

Chapter 9    A Glorious Day .............................. 45

Chapter 10   Camp ........................................ 52

Chapter 11   Here and There .............................. 57

             Postscript .................................. 62

# Foreword

On many occasions over the years, I have had the privilege to teach the story of Amy Carmichael's life, which has been a great inspiration to millions of people around the world.

Two years ago I was teaching her story in five episodes to the Adventures' club at Kilkeel Baptist Tabernacle. I highlighted her early life in Northern Ireland and then told of how she rescued the Temple children in India.

At the end of one of these meetings, Megan Gordon, an eight-year-old girl, came to me and said, "I want to be saved."

Another girl called Amy also attended those Amy Carmichael lessons and listened to every word. She was a Christian and the end of the first lesson, she told me that she wanted to be a missionary like Amy Carmichael.

The simple lessons of Amy's life prompted me to enquire if conditions had improved for young girls in India's temples or if they still needed to be rescued as in Amy's day. I knew a law had been passed in 1948 prohibiting child-prostitution in those Buddhist temples. Even though that law was reviewed in 1982, I discovered that although this law is on the statute books, it is largely ignored and the police turn a blind eye to crime or are even involved in it.

I was invited to speak at several meetings in which I highlighted the story of Amy and the continuing and worsening plight of "temple girls" in India. At those meetings, I asked the ladies to pray for these abused and neglected children.

One day while I was praying about how I could help missionaries in India, Mrs Joan Patton, a friend from my church, said to me, "Did you know that Bertha McNally was a missionary in India?" After my involvement with Child Evangelism Fellowship for many years, I thought I knew Bertha well. This was news to me, and I enquired if anybody had ever written her life story.

When the answer was negative, I said to Joan, "I'm going to ask Bertha would she let me write down her story." Hence this book.

When I went to see Bertha in her home, she was sitting as calm, regal and wise as a queen on a throne. I could not believe she was 93 for I could find no wrinkles on her rosy cheeks, only laughter lines around her bright blue, smiling eyes.

While we chatted, she told me that she had kept a notebook down through the years in which she had written quotes that had spoken to her heart. I discovered that her notebook contained the most beautiful, neat and clear handwriting.

When I asked Bertha if she would allow me to write her life story, she said, "Oh, no one would want to read about my life. I'm just an ordinary person."

I replied, "We are all ordinary people Bertha, but with God, we can do extraordinary things."

Here is the story of an extraordinary life.

**Christine Bell**

CHAPTER 1

# The Livingstons

It was only since 1975 that the folks of Kilkeel, Co. Down, came to hear of Mrs Bertha McNally. It was then that she and her husband Sammy arrived from Lurgan to be the first couple to oversee the work at "Seaview," the Child Evangelism Fellowship Camp House on the Harbour Road. Before their marriage in 1968, Bertha was known in Lurgan as Roberta Livingston, a missionary to India.

Bertha was born Grace Roberta Livingston (pronounced Livingstone), the youngest of eight children, on 27th May 1923, to Robert and Annie (nee Stone). Their first family home was at Moyraverty, located between Portadown and Lurgan.

Bertha had the great privilege to be reared in a Christian home. Mr Livingston, a shoemaker by trade, was also the Sunday School Superintendent at the local Brethren Hall. This meant that from a very early age Bertha heard the gospel and knew the way of salvation. At the tender age of four, she gave her heart to the Lord Jesus Christ. Although she was only a child, she had the blessed assurance that Christ was in her heart and life. That early step moulded and determined the course of her life for the next ninety years.

This was not only a godly family; it was also a very happy home, which created lots of pleasant memories. However, family life suddenly changed when Mr Livingston suffered a stroke that left him an invalid.

The family suffered another major setback when Mrs Livingston went to visit her daughter Annie and her husband Bobby McAfee in their new home in Bangor. Mrs Livingston had been helping to make a rockery in the garden. After a while, she returned to the house and said to her daughter, "Annie, I'm going to die." With that, the mother collapsed at her daughter's feet. Annie was stunned for her mother had died very suddenly. The doctor described her heart as being threadbare. She was only fifty-three years of age.

Years earlier Mrs Livingston had suffered the loss of a child but was able to raise seven other children as well as caring for her invalid husband. Although life had been hard for Mrs Livingston and was cut short, she had been ready to meet the Lord.

After the death of her mother even though Bertha was only twelve years old, she took up the responsibility of caring for her father until he died aged sixty-three. Mr Livingston was a godly, Christian gentleman. He was greatly loved by his family and highly respected by all who knew him.

Following her father's death, Bertha, at the age of eighteen, found employment at the stationary counter of the popular F. W. Woolworth's shop in the town. She loved organizing the materials, keeping everything tidy and displayed the products very neatly.

Bertha's older sister, Lily, also worked at Woolworths. Although Lily worked upstairs in the stock room, she always looked out for Bertha and treated her more like a mother than a sister.

Two years later, in 1943, aged twenty, Bertha left home and employment in Woolworths to go to England. This was the beginning of her four years nursing and midwifery training at St. Luke's Hospital in Bradford.

A kind Christian lady in Bradford, Mrs Joan Pickles, opened her home to give Bertha lodgings during her training years in England. Bertha's sister Lily said that if Bertha hadn't left home, her brothers would never have married because she took such good care of them.

Lily also gave up her employment at Woolworths to go to the Faith Mission Bible College in Edinburgh. After her training, Lily worked with the Faith Mission in Donegal. While there, Lily saw an appeal for missionaries in India. God used that appeal to call Lily to serve Him with the Poona Indian Village Mission (P.I.V.M.) in that vast sub-continent.

Consequently, in 1945, Lily left her family, her close friends, and work with the Faith Mission to serve the Lord in India. Because her departure was at the end of World War II, Lily travelled on a blacked-out ship because of the risk of being torpedoed during the voyage to India. Thankfully, she arrived safely in Bombay, now Mumbai. From there she continued her journey overland by train and cart. When the new missionary from Lurgan finally arrived at the P.I.V.M. mission compound, she was presented to the lady-missionary in charge who said to Lily, "From now on you will be called Elizabeth!"

In 1947 Bertha finished her training at St. Luke's Hospital in Bradford as a qualified nurse and midwife.

Following the completion of her training, Bertha began working as a district nurse on the outskirts of Glasgow, Scotland. For this, she acquired a car to enable her to travel around the countryside. Bertha enjoyed living in her lovely little cottage where she was supplied with free coal. While living there, she attended the local Gospel Hall.

The 27th May 1950, Bertha's birthday, was a dark and dismal day, pouring down with rain. Bertha decided to drive the twenty miles to visit a couple that had been Faith Mission pilgrims before they were married. During her visit, they discussed with her the possibility of Bertha serving the Lord in some capacity in the future. God had already been stirring Bertha to surrender more to Him. With this conversation, she was spurred about her willingness to give up employment, step out in faith to study at a Bible College.

Bertha left her friends' home that day with four information leaflets about four different Bible Colleges. After three years in Scotland Bertha decided to return home to Lurgan to take time to think more about her future and God's plan for her life

CHAPTER 2

# Family Business or the Father's Business

While Bertha was at home in Lurgan, praying for God to guide her next step, her brothers, Charlie and Wycliffe, asked her to work for them in their local grocery shop. The shop was a large building with an imposing sign displayed outside, "Livingston Brothers." Bertha was impressed with her two brothers who looked very smart in their clean white coats.

Every Thursday big barrels of pork were delivered to the shop from Portadown and soon queues of people lined outside the shop wanting to buy pork. In those days pig's knees and trotters (feet) were very popular. Bertha remembers the ladies asking, "Have you any knees, Mr Livingston?"

Either of the brothers always gave the same answer, "Yes ladies, plenty of knees."

Later, Bertha went to work for her brothers when they opened a new shop in Ballywalter, Co Down. There she sold petrol besides the general grocery products. While working in Ballywalter, Bertha's brother, Wycliffe, met his future wife, Ruby Wilson. He and Ruby were married in Ballywalter Gospel Hall, and Bertha was the happy bridesmaid for that special day.

Bertha's brothers recognised the great help, and ability Bertha had given them in managing their shops, and out of gratitude, they wanted to set her up with her own shop. With that in mind, they thought that a baby clothes' shop would be just perfect for her. In fact, the shop they had their mind on was the very same shop their mother Annie had rented when she was a young woman. However, Bertha wasn't interested in managing shops nor was she interested in having her own business or making lots of money. After these two years of seeking the Lord's guidance, Bertha knew what the next step should be.

In 1952 Bertha left home again for Mount Hermon Bible and Missionary Training College in Ealing, England. Mount Hermon was an all-female college and Bertha had enrolled for a two-year course there. The corresponding all-male college was known as "All Nations Bible College." The two colleges later merged to become the present day "All Nations Bible College" north of London.

At that time Miss Irene Crockren was the Principal at Mount Hermon Bible College. One crucial question she asked all the new girls on their arrival was, "How will you meet your fees?"

Although Bertha felt very nervous, she answered with a little confidence, "I worked for my brothers, and they put money into a bank account for me, so I have my fees." Meanwhile, the other new arrivals were in the hallway talking about "praying in their fees." At that time Bertha didn't understand what they were talking about.

While Bertha was working for her brothers and thinking about Bible College, her sister Elizabeth in India had met Errol Pattenmore, a handsome young man who was also a missionary with the Poona Indian Village Mission. They married in November 1951.

Elizabeth wrote to Bertha from India saying she believed that Bertha would approve of her choice of a husband. Elizabeth was right. Two years later, in October 1953, baby Stephen Pattenmore was born. A few years later, another little boy was added to the family, Philip Pattenmore.

At Mount Hermon Miss Crockren had another very important question to ask Bertha and the other girls; "Where will you go to serve the Lord when your time at Bible College is over?"

Once again Bertha had a rush of nerves. She answered, "I don't know about any other country other than India because my sister Lily is a missionary there."

Miss Crockren smiled and replied, "Is it not just like the Lord to call two sisters to the same country." These words were not only a great encouragement to Bertha; they were guidance for her. Now she knew what she must do.

As Bertha's plans for going to India began to develop, she thought of the words of William Carey, (the recognised "Father of the Modern Missionary Movement") before he ventured to India, "I will go down into the pit if you will 'hold the ropes.'" Carey was referring to Acts 9:25 when Paul's friends held the ropes as they lowered him down the Damascus walls in a basket. Carey's friends replied, "While we live, we will never let go of the ropes."

Bertha's friends and members of her home church in Lurgan also pledged to "hold the ropes" for her wherever God would send her – in India and later in Seaview. Even when Bertha retired in her nineties, her friends from

Lurgan continued to "hold the ropes" by prayer support and practical help.

Bertha wrote to her sister Lily every week. It was a momentous day when she sent a letter saying, "I'm coming to work with you in India." That was in January 1954.

CHAPTER 3

# India

In 1298, Marco Polo wrote, "India is the richest and most splendid province in the world." This vast country India had been part of the British Empire and governed by Britain from 1600 until the nation won its independence in 1947 after a fierce struggle, which lasted for more than fifty years. Today India is still rich in natural beauty, plentiful wildlife, cultural traditions, various crafts and many trades. However, many areas are still impoverished because of primitive agriculture, inefficient industry, and multiple problems of illiteracy, boorish traditions, malnutrition, and disease. Bertha had heard of all these difficult and dangerous circumstances in India, but she, like Elizabeth, was going there to share the good news of the Gospel of Christ.

The disciple Thomas was the first missionary to take Christianity to India in the middle of the first century. Thomas had also evangelized the edges of China, Burma (Myanmar) and Malaysia before arriving in South India. He landed at Kodungallur on the Malabar Coast, which is present-day Kerala. Thomas preached the Gospel to the Brahmin families, and many of them became Christians. Between 52 and 59 AD, he founded seven churches;

Kodungallur, Kottakkaru, Palayur, Kollam, Kokkaman-galam, Niranam and Chayil. These churches today belong to the Malankara Mar Thomas Nasranis movement.

In AD 67 Thomas moved to the east coast of India. There the Braham priests of Mylapore feared Christianity would eclipse Hinduism. Consequently, an Indian King, whose wife had become a Christian, ordered his high priest to kill Thomas. The great apostle and pioneer missionary was martyred in 72 AD, he died of stab wounds. He was buried in Mylapore, which is near Chennai.

Bertha and Elizabeth were not the only members of the Livingston family to emigrate. After selling his grocery shop, Charlie immigrated to Australia where he continued in the grocery business. In 1956 Elizabeth and her family were able to visit Charlie in Australia during their furlough from India.

After the sale of their grocery shop in Lurgan, Wycliffe opened another shop selling greeting cards. Wycliffe was greatly loved by everyone who knew him, especially by Bertha. One day a missionary met Wycliffe and challenged him, "Wycliffe, Don't waste your time selling cards, the unsaved can do that. Go and do work for the Lord".

Wycliffe and his wife Ruby responded to that challenge, and after spending three years at Bible College, they left Lurgan to serve God as missionaries in Peru. During their forty years serving the Lord in South America, God greatly blessed Wycliffe, and he saw much fruit for his labours.

Later in life, Wycliffe and Ruby ran a retirement home in British Colombia, Canada. They finally retired to Salt Spring Island where Elizabeth's son Stephen, was able to visit them in 2011. After a very full and fulfilling life

Wycliffe passed away in October 2012 aged 94 and Ruby in September 2014. They were greatly loved and sadly missed.

Early in 1954, Bertha boarded the Belfast to Liverpool boat, Caledonia, and then on to India. That journey was an amazing experience for Bertha. Every day took her farther from home but each day brought new adventures. After several weeks she arrived in the bustling city of Bombay. For Bertha, the sights, sounds, and smells of the Orient were simply from an alien world; the blazing sun, the relentless heat and the vast numbers of people moving to and fro like colourful ants, were quite overwhelming.

On closer inspection, terrible poverty was exposed. Bertha was appalled to see such stark poverty and painful anguish. She felt the distress was heart breaking. At the same time she knew that was why she had come to India. She had come to make a difference.

Like her sister Lily years earlier, Bertha took the train from Bombay to Poona (today is known as Puna) and to the P.I.V.M. mission station there. When Bertha finally found Elizabeth's house inside the mission compound, there was such a joyful and tearful welcome and reunion. With great excitement and relief the two sisters hugged each other. This was followed by introductions and hugs from Elizabeth's husband, Errol Pattenmore.

Although Bertha was exhausted from her travels, she was too excited to sleep. The two sisters stayed awake all night until breakfast time, talking with each other about family, friends and all that had transpired in the intervening years since last they met. They had so much to catch up on.

Both sisters recognised that it was so wonderful that they could work together for their Lord and Master in that needy land of India and were grateful for the opportunity to do so. Bertha's skills as a nurse and midwife were a great help and blessing to the work of the Poona Mission.

Australian missionary Charles Reeve founded the Poona Indian Village Mission. He was a Tasmanian farmer and evangelist. He later became a Baptist pastor in 1893. In 1900, just seven years after the P.I.V.M. was started, cholera and bubonic plague, along with a famine, which came as a result of the failure of the monsoon rains, killed tens of thousands of people. The famine and diseases swept through the whole of India, leaving the nation devastated.

The P.I.V.M. employed 1,000 people to help in the relief work during which their four hundred missionaries supplied food for the starving Indians. The Mission's nurses cared for those dying of the bubonic plague.

In 1968, the P.I.V.M. merged with "Ceylon and India General Mission", to become the "International Christian Fellowship" (I.C.F.). Subsequently, the I.C.F. merged with "Serving in Mission" (S.I.M.).

After their long night of conversation it was time for the two ladies to get some sleep and nourishment. After that, they had to attend to the newly arrived missionary's luggage. Bertha had brought one big trunk. When she had unpacked, the other missionaries were aghast. They said, "Oh, Bertha has brought so little for herself – everything else in the trunk is for Elizabeth and others. She has no clothes for herself."

On the next day Bertha was taken to the dressmaker to have clothes made with light, cool material because of the sweltering weather. There were lots of things Bertha had to get used to. There was not only the climate and the Indian cuisine. There was this new sounding Marathi language, which was very strange to her ear. She knew it was most important to get to know the Indian people, but she could not do this without learning their native tongue.

Elizabeth had a messenger boy called Sudecka, and on Bertha's first day she heard Elizabeth give some instructions to him in the Marathi. Bertha felt frustrated that she didn't understand what her sister had said. This made Bertha more determined to learn the language. Very soon she would have the opportunity.

Bertha was sent straight away to the hill station of Mahableshar for language study. Mahableshar was 75 miles (120 km) from the P.I.V.M. mission headquarters in Poona. Although the initial two years were given over to language study, that was only the beginning. Marathi, the language of Maharashra, is closely related to Hindi that is spoken by around thirty per cent of the Indian population. India has the second largest population in the world. Some eighty-two per cent of Indians are Hindus; eighteen per cent are Buddhists, Sikhs, Muslims, and Christians.

After Bertha had learned some of the language, she let it be known that she needed someone to help her and work for her. Indian men soon crowded round her, hoping for employment, but she didn't know whom to pick. One man shouted out, "I can burn the bread." Bertha hired him immediately because he had the very important skill of making "toast."

The first mention of Bertha in the P.I.V.M magazine was in the July- September issue of 1954. It was a write-up wishing to congratulate "Miss Grace Roberta Livingston on the passing of her second language exam."

The magazine indicated that Bertha was assigned to work at the boys' orphanage and baby boys' home in Nasrapur, 22 miles (36 km) from Poona. Bertha not only became a nurse to these children but a mother to them.

While Bertha was posted at Nasrapur, Elizabeth had frequent contact with her since she was living in the mission headquarters in Poona where Errol was the Field Secretary for P.I.V.M. in India. Stephen and Philip, Bertha's nephews, remember auntie Bertha as a very "doting auntie."

Philip later said that "between medical help and parenting the Indian children, Bertha took great care of those little boys, many of them being just toddlers and babies." On one occasion when Phillip was only twelve years old, while on holiday from boarding school, he spent a short time with Bertha in Nasrapur. While there Bertha introduced Philip to a little five-year-old boy. The boy had hypothyroidism and was very intellectually delayed. His parents had given him the Marathi name for 'parrot', which was considered to be an unclean or despised bird. This was done to either avoid undue attention from the gods or because he had been cursed by the gods.

Bertha renamed the boy "Robin" and maintained him on thyroid replacement medication. Sadly, this was too late to help his mental development. During the entirety of Philip's holiday, he took care of little Robin.

Bertha gave Philip her collection of Handel's Messiah records. Thereafter, Philip played them day and night and learned to sing all the parts. During Philip's visit Bertha often took Phillip and the children into the woods for picnics, taking the gramophone with them.

Also during one of Philip's visits to auntie Bertha there was a 6.5 magnitude earthquake in the Poonar region. Bertha ended up giving earthquake drills for the boys in the middle of the night. She got them up and brought them outside to rehearse their drills. Phillip always made sure Robin was with him.

Those visits to auntie Bertha became part of the wonderful memories of Philip and Stephen's childhood in India.

# CHAPTER 4

# Curtains and Looms

Some years later, Bertha was posted at the P.I.V.M. mission station and hospital in Pandharpur, which was a major Hindu pilgrimage site. As a nurse, Bertha's main responsibility was to care for the little children who were in need of medical attention. However, Bertha had another very important role.

She and another missionary nurse, along with two Indian ladies, travelled by jeep to set up a clinic in a certain location. Usually, the best place for this was under a group of leafy trees, which provided shade for the mobile team and their weary and sick patients. At these locations between twenty to forty leprosy patients of all ages listened to the Gospel being preached by the two Indian ladies. The patients then received their medical treatment from Bertha and her Australian or American colleague.

Late in 1959 to mid-1960, Bertha was home on furlough. While visiting her sister Annie in Bangor, Annie insisted that Bertha would take back to India, Annie's enormous heavy, black, embossed curtains complete with their black linings. They were from her big bay window and had been used for the obligatory blackouts during the war. Bertha didn't want to take them. How could I carry them all the way to India and of what use would they be there anyway? So she thought. However, to please her sister, Bertha returned to India with this huge bundle of curtain material.

Bertha was assigned back to the junior boys' hostel in Nasrapur to relieve her missionary friend, Miss Hooper. To her horror she found that there were around thirty-five sick little boys suffering from measles waiting for auntie Bertha to arrive. The particular strain of measles threatened to cause blindness or brain damage to the children. Bertha says she still remembers the eyes of the ill children and described their eyes as looking like they were "floating in blood."

Because sunlight was very dangerous for their condition, one of the first things Bertha had to do after administering the proper medicines was to hang Annie's big black curtains on the windows to keep out the very strong and bright Indian sunlight.

Many of these young boys were orphans or had been abandoned. Others had parents or family in the village, but they were too poor to provide for their children. These deprived and destitute boys found a loving home and a warm family in the hostel where they were fed, clothed, educated and taught the Scriptures. Added to this they also received the best medical attention and great affection from Auntie Bertha.

The boys from the junior hostel were between the ages of one to eleven. The senior boys' hostel for the twelve to eighteen-year-olds was located in the next field. After the age of eighteen, the missionaries arranged employment for the young men to support themselves and help their families.

Bertha thought of a way that her boys could acquire a much needed and useful skill. She wanted them to learn how to hand weave. Bertha was their teacher, but she also needed to learn how to hand weave. Bertha went to stay with Mrs Robertson, an Australian missionary who taught Bertha how to produce work on the handloom.

After only one week of tuition, Bertha bought a handloom and was carrying it home with her. When she was about to board a train, she discovered it was a tight squeeze and a little embarrassment to get the loom through the door and into the carriage. She finally managed it.

Back at the hostel, Bertha wasted no time asking the carpenter to make three more looms, using the bought loom as a template. While they waited for the looms to be ready, Bertha made a big folding blind for the veranda to provide shade from the strong Indian sun. That meant that the veranda was the coolest place to hold the class. She discovered later that the folds of the blind were also a perfect place for little pink baby mice.

Child by child, Bertha taught the boys how to use this new contraption, the loom. With much patience and determination, by both teacher and pupil, they learned to hand-weave table runners and placemats. Bertha later sent these to Ireland to be sold. The money earned was spent on more yarn to produce more weaves, and so their profitable work continued.

Bertha had trained them and provided the young boys with skilful crafts that would be useful and profitable after they left the hostel.

Bertha's grandfather worked a handloom in his home as part of the cottage industry. Also, her brother Bobby taught textiles at Lurgan Technical College. It seemed as though sewing talents had been in the family genes. Over the years that followed Bertha made more than twenty quilts.

Bertha was a very gifted lady.

CHAPTER 5

# Out of the Blue

Someone else thought that Bertha was a very special lady. On 1st April 1968 while still in India, Bertha received a letter from Ireland 'out of the blue.' That letter would change the course of her life.

The author of the letter was Mr Sammy McNally, and it contained a proposal of marriage. When Bertha received this 'proposition' as Sammy called it, she was so shocked that she cried. She was over-whelmed by Sammy's declaration of his love for her. It had been a love that was unspoken until the letter arrived. Now Bertha had it in black and white.

While Bertha had been home doing her deputation work to represent the Mission, Sammy volunteered to take Bertha to the meetings. No one seemed to think anything about it, but Sammy obviously did. He had loved Bertha from their early days together when they met in Lurgan at the Band Room. Bertha loved Sammy then, but it never developed.

When Bertha left home at twenty years old, she would be virtually absent from Lurgan for the next twenty-five years. Now she was forty-five years old, and Sammy was five years older than her. He was born 26th April 1918, to

Thomas and Matilda McNally. His brothers and sisters were Thomas, Willie, John, Elizabeth (Mrs Marshall) and Jane (Mrs Crozier). They were reared at 46, Hill Street, Lurgan.

Although Bertha was born at Moyrafferty in 1923, her family left there in 1928 and moved to Hill Street in Lurgan. Bertha's aunt, Gracie Ann, was the sister of Bertha's father. Gracie Ann lived and stayed on at the family home in Hill Street to look after her parents and her brothers until they married and left home.

Aunt Gracie Ann, as Lily had also done, advised Bertha to follow a career and not to stay at home to look after her brothers. Her aunt said to Bertha, "Brothers go away and get married, and you are left alone in the end." Gracie Ann never married, and she didn't want that to happen to Bertha. When Gracie Ann died, the old family home of Hill Street was left to Bertha's father, Robert.

Sammy lived at one end of Hill Street and Bertha at the other, with the hill in the middle. Amazingly, as children, they had never met and did not know each other until 1938, when the evangelist Tom Rees arrived in Lurgan for special evangelistic meetings.

Many young people including Sammy McNally were converted at that evangelistic mission. He was twenty years old. Bertha was only fifteen at the time she got to know Sammy and the young people who had come to Christ.

When they met, Sammy soon realized that Bertha was a very strong Christian. He soon developed a burden to work for God among these teenagers and children. He wanted to help them grow and mature in their newfound faith. With that in mind, he said to Bertha, "What are we going to do with all these young ones?"

Bertha must have had good ideas as the work they had initiated at the Band Room became a thriving children's work in Sloan Street, Lurgan. Sammy rented "the Band. Room" for one shilling a week. The Band Room was a dilapidated shack with a sagging roof and was so named because it was there that the Hill Street Band practiced. Sammy and Bertha taught the Word of God each week in that old hall, and Bertha played the organ.

Sammy also started a young people's fellowship, which met above the central café in the town. The work grew, and Sammy soon had the young people involved with open-air meetings and preaching engagements.

After five years, Bertha had to leave Sammy and the work at the band room to go to England to begin her nursing training. Although five years her senior, Sammy had become her best friend and was like a brother to her. They laughed and cried together and played and prayed together. They knew that with Bertha's departure they would miss their close friendship and fellowship.

Sammy McNally's zeal for God and His work in Lurgan and beyond were legendary. He was frequently invited to preach at churches and mission halls all over the countryside. Alan Little, a friend of Sammy's, related how Sammy was invited to preach at a venue in Londonderry, a distance of almost one hundred miles from Lurgan. After Sammy had travelled quite a distance, he noticed that the fuel gauge on the car was almost at empty. He feared he had not enough fuel to reach his destination and he was virtually penniless. Instead of thinking any more about his sermon for that night, Sammy prayed all the way until he finally he arrived at the church. The pressure was off for he knew he would receive some money from the church for his travel expenses. He was so thankful to God for answered prayer.

After preaching at the meeting, he enjoyed some supper and plenty of conversation with the church friends. To his dismay, although the church friends bade him "Good night," no one mentioned to him about his travelling expenses or gave him any money. If Sammy had prayed to keep the car going until he got to the church, you could only imagine how he prayed until he arrived home in Lurgan, and he did. Sammy maintained that the car made it on faith and fumes.

With his enthusiasm for the youth in Lurgan Sammy decided to organise a summer camp at Drumgore near Lurgan. He acquired a farmyard and soon had a team of volunteers cleaning out the mess of the pig houses, wash and whitewash walls to provide accommodation for the campers. The rustic barn was used for their dining hall and meetings while cooking was done in the open-air. Sammy advertised the camp in national Christian magazines and soon had a great response from England, Scotland and Northern Ireland.

The camp was a memorable week for all who attended. When the young people ran and played in the fields they had to be careful they didn't tumble into what the cows had left behind. Inevitably, some did.

Sammy led the Bible studies each morning and evening. Joe Wright, former missionary to Brazil, showed a missionary film one night. When the lights went out, Joe hollered the call of Amazon Indians in the dark and frightened the life out of the young people. As he showed the movie the projector's reel could not wind in the film, so it just spilled all over the floor. Joe had to rewind the film unto the spool at the end of the meeting. That was a memorable night of fun and challenge.

At the end of the week, several young people trusted the Saviour. Furthermore, many young Christians surrendered and rededicated their lives to Christ. The camp and the continuing work at the Sloan Street Band Room resulted in quite a few of those young people going to bible colleges and into the Lord's work at home and abroad.

Twenty-five years had passed since Bertha had left Lurgan before receiving this proposal for marriage from a very patient Sammy McNally. Although it was a very pleasant shock for Bertha, it presented her with a big dilemma. She never thought Sammy would ever ask her to leave the mission field. She had no idea what to think or what to do next.

When Bertha read the letter, she was the only staff member on duty at the hostel that night. Everyone else was away for the Easter holidays. Bertha sat on the veranda in the cool of that evening. There was no one else to speak to other than Toby, her pet collie dog. The perplexed dog looked quizzically up at Bertha as she told all about Sammy's 'out of the blue' marriage idea.

When the other staff members returned, it was Bertha's time to take a short break. She decided to visit Elsie Foster, an Australian missionary colleague who lived quite a distance away. Elsie was a single girl and had been sick for some time and eventually died of cancer.

The two ladies were glad to see each other again. After a warm welcome with tight embraces followed by a cup of tea, Bertha began to open her heart and tell Elsie all about the surprise letter from Lurgan. Elsie was as overwhelmed as Bertha with the fantastic news and was just as excited too.

"Have you given Sammy your answer yet?" Elsie asked.

"Not yet," answered Bertha, "for I don't know the answer myself."

Elsie was forthright; "Well, my girl, when you get back to the hostel, go into your room and pray, pray, pray! Don't come out of that room until you do know the answer and then write to the man and tell him."

That's exactly what Bertha did. As she prayed, she was assured that the answer should be a resounding 'yes' to Sammy's 'proposition.' After thirty years of close friendship, Bertha Livingston resolved that she would marry Sammy McNally.

# CHAPTER 6

# A New Beginning

After Bertha had ascertained what her answer to Sammy's proposition should be, she lost no time in eagerly putting pen to paper to give her affirmative reply. She had experienced many of India's infamous tropical cyclones, but the brewing up of this romantic storm was sweeping her off her feet. Her excitement at the prospect of marriage was mingled with sadness and heartbreak at the thought of leaving her beautiful and beloved India. Over her fifteen years of devoted service for the Lord in India, she had fallen in love with the country, the people and especially the dear children in the hostels. It was hard to leave all of this behind. Bertha wept as she said her farewells to her missionary colleagues and many Indian friends.

However, this was not a time for looking back with any regrets. Although she was forty-five years old and Sammy was fifty, they were sure that God still had a great future for them.

Since Bertha had sent her positive reply to Sammy, her head was filled with thoughts of how she would plan their wedding. As news of their forthcoming marriage filtered among their friends, there was great surprise and delight. There were plenty of messages of support, good wishes and kind offers to help them, but Bertha and Sammy didn't want any fuss. At the same time, they had to make plans and preparation for their special day.

As the time for the wedding approached a particular friend of Bertha's spied a lovely light blue suit in a shop window that was on sale for half of its original price. Immediately she thought that if the suit fitted her, it would also fit Bertha. In the shop, she tried on the garment and found that it fitted her perfectly. She promptly bought the outfit and could hardly wait to tell the bride-to-be about the bargain.

Bertha was taken aback by the kind and unexpected gift of the suit and greatly appreciated the thoughtfulness of this helpful friend. Subsequently, Bertha was able to find a beautiful blue hat that was a perfect match for the wedding outfit.

To avoid too many people turning up to see this spectacle of two middle-aged people tying the knot Bertha and Sammy decided to be married at Richview Presbyterian Church in Belfast. Bertha explained, "The 'world and his wife' would have been out to see them for Sammy was so well known and loved."

Their special day was 31st August 1968. Sammy's very close friend, Alfie Bell, who was his best man, congratulated the "young couple" that had waited a quarter of a century for God's time to come together.

The newly-weds settled in Lurgan for the first eighteen months. During that time Bertha worked in the Andrew Brothers' wallpaper and paint shop. In May 1969 her sister Elizabeth travelled from New Zealand to visit her young sister and to become better acquainted with her new brother-in-law. Elizabeth thought this might be her last visit to Northern Ireland as her husband, Errol Pattenmore, had agreed to take up the position of the Mission's representative in New Zealand.

Elizabeth's visit was unforgettable as the two sisters had so much in common – their lives with their siblings in Lurgan, the years in India and the memory of many mutual friends and colleagues. Above all, they were thrilled and excited about the forthcoming wedding, especially when Elizabeth had almost been resigned to the fact their sister Bertha would be a spinster for the rest of her life.

Sammy retold to Elizabeth the story of his secret love for Bertha. After Bertha went to Bradford for nursing training, Sammy enrolled at the Faith Mission Training Home in Edinburgh. After two years there he worked with the Faith Mission travelling all over Ireland with a mobile bookshop, distributing Gospel literature and conducting Prayer Unions in the evenings.

During those days with the Faith Mission, he knew that he was in love with Bertha Livingston, but he did not want to stand in her way of following her sister Elizabeth to the mission field. His restraint was difficult, but he had resolved in his heart not to mention his feelings for her lest he should hinder or divert her. Bertha knew nothing of this closely guarded secret love.

After his work with the Faith Mission Sammy returned to Lurgan where he put all his efforts into the work of Child Evangelism Fellowship (CEF) in the town and the North Armagh area.

When he returned to Lurgan Sammy found employment at Fred Wilson's General Merchants business. He later

*May 1937, Bertha aged 15 at Hill Street Lurgan*

*Miss Bertha Livingston, aged 24, on her graduation on completing her training as a nurse/midwife in 1947.*

*Bertha enjoying Spring*

Sammy at work in Ireland while Bertha is in India.

David McQuilken the then Director of CEF Ireland invited Sammy & Bertha to run Seaview.

Sammy and Bertha on their wedding day with bridesmaid, Ethel Trotter and best man, Alfie Bell

*Seaview on the Harbour Road, Kilkeel.*

*Sammy and Bertha having devotionals together*

*Decorating Seaview purchased by CEF in 1975.*

*Sandra Watts (Shields) joined Sammy and Bertha at Seaview when only 16.*

*Sammy and Bertha with Amy McBurney. Amy retired from Nepal after serving the Lord there for 28 years.*

*Sammy at the chips*

*Bertha at work in the kitchen at Seaview*

*Henry Berry with camp children at Seaview*

*The Seaview Good News Club*

*Des and Margaret Wright who took over from Sammy and Bertha in 1982*

*Sammy and Bertha outside Seaview*

*Mrs Patton*

*Joan Patton*

*Madge and Bobby Graham with Bertha*

*Bertha on her 94th Birthday at Slieve Roe House*

moved to Pinewood Products (picture framers). Years earlier Sammy had wanted to serve God as a missionary in South America, but this ambition was frustrated when he fell victim to tuberculosis. Consequently, he underwent thoracic surgery, which left him with one functioning lung. This condition resulted in invalidating any plans for Sammy living or working abroad.

Even though Sammy had only one lung, he continued his employment at Fred Wilson's. The other men with whom he worked complained that they couldn't keep up with him. He was not only a hard worker; he also had a great sense of humour a happy smile and always had a pleasant disposition. Everyone looked up to Sammy as a true gentleman and a genuinely godly person.

While Bertha was still working at Andrews' shop, her friend, Esther Poots, told her about a job she believed would suit Bertha perfectly, a sales assistant at a local Christian bookshop. Armed with this information Bertha phoned the owner of the bookshop enquiring about the position. The manager, Mrs Best, went to Andrews' shop to meet Bertha personally and speak to her about the position. Mrs Best took an immediate liking to Bertha and offered her the job.

During the interview, Mrs Best hadn't mentioned anything about wages, but that was no problem to Bertha for money was not the most important thing in her life. However, at the end of the week, much to Bertha's surprise, she discovered that the new job provided her with a pay increase. Sammy also benefitted from Bertha's move to the Christian bookshop. He read all the books so that Bertha was able to recommend them to her customers. The

Lurgan Christian bookshop later passed to become one of the Faith Mission's chain of Christian bookshops.

After their marriage, Sammy and Bertha continued to be fully involved in the local CEF work. On one occasion while they were conducting the Good News Club at the Band Room, a bashful little boy, escaped by going through Sammy's legs, and ran home. He obviously didn't want to attend the meetings. That little boy was Andy Burns.

Although Andy's shyness made him try to avoid those early children's meetings at the Band Room, when he was eighteen years old, he began to attend the Church of Ireland in Lurgan. One Sunday evening a friend invited Andy to go with him to Lurgan Baptist Church to hear Pastor Willie Mullan preach. On that night both Andy and his friend trusted the Lord as their Saviour. The man who counselled the two young men and led them to the Lord also suggested they might help at a Good News Club at Mourne View housing estate on the following Monday night.

Even though these two lads were new converts, they turned up to help at the meeting that Monday evening. After that, they went to the Good News Club every week and became so enthusiastic about reaching boys and girls for Christ that they branched out to start up several other clubs in the Lurgan area.

In time the Lord called Andy to go to Bible College where he studied for three years. After that, he spent three more months studying at the CEF Training Institute in Kilzimmer, Switzerland. Andy was assigned to do his practical training with CEF in Northern Ireland's Mourne area.

While working in the Mournes, Andy met and married Marina Campbell, a nurse from Kilkeel. Soon after their wedding Andy and Marina left the Mournes to continue their work with CEF in Dundee, Scotland. While they were there, they developed an outreach ministry to young people who roamed the streets of Dundee each night.

During their twenty years in Dundee, many young people were rescued from wasteful lives and are now following the Saviour.

Due to family commitments, Marina's father, Bertie Campbell, will be one hundred years old this June, Andy, and Marina had to return to Kilkeel. Although they have changed location, Andy continues to organise the outreach work in Dundee, returning to there every month. In Northern Ireland, Andy engages in a similar street ministry in Kilkeel, Newcastle, Warrenpoint and in his hometown of Lurgan. He has also helped start a special work team among the youth in Armagh Baptist Church. Marina, who is a great support and encouragement to Andy, works at the local Brooklands Nursing Home.

Andy and Marina's Christian ministry is only one example of the many young people who were called into Christian work because of Sammy McNally's devotion to reaching young people for the Saviour and motivating them to engage in the Lord's work.

## CHAPTER 7

# Seaview

In April 1975, almost seven years after they had tied the knot and settled into their busy round of work and Christian outreach in Lurgan, David and Mollie McQuilken, National Directors of CEF Ireland, arrived at the McNally's Hill Street home. It was not unusual for David and Mollie to visit the McNallys. Like Sammy and Bertha, the McQuilkens also came from Lurgan, and both couples shared their mutual concern to reach boys and girls with the Gospel.

CEF work in Ireland had started in 1950 with the first Good News Club in the home of Sam and Sadie Doherty at Bleary, not far from Lurgan. The first CEF open-air meetings in Lurgan and Portadown commenced soon after that. Sam and Sadie Doherty were National Directors until 1964 when they left Ireland to lead the CEF work in Europe. It was then that David and Mollie who had been working with Sam and Sadie from the early days of the work took their place as full-time National Directors of CEF in Ireland. Until then David had been a teacher at the local Lurgan Technical College. The Lord blessed their leadership and the work in Ireland was experiencing great growth.

After the initial greetings, David announced that he and Mollie were visiting them with a specific purpose in mind. David proceeded to tell Sammy and Bertha about an opportunity for CEF to purchase "Seaview," a large property on the Harbour Road in Kilkeel. The previous owners of "Seaview," Mr and Mrs Harris, had previously used their large property as their bed and breakfast business. CEF workers had already used the Seaview facilities for children's camps during the previous three years. Now the Mr and Mrs Harris wanted to sell their house and retire.

The members of the National Committee of CEF were keen to buy the property and to make it a permanent Christian camp centre for children. However, they needed a suitable couple to manage it and be house parents to the boys and girls. David and Molly told the McNallys that they had been praying for God's guidance in the matter and as a result, they were persuaded that God had put Sammy and Bertha on their hearts.

It is easy to understand why David and Mollie were guided to approach Sammy and Bertha. Besides being a dedicated Christian worker, Sammy was able to turn his hand to many useful skills. Added to this, Bertha's missionary experience made her an ideal person to be a house parent for the children.

After some discussion, Sammy and Bertha asked David to give them time to seek God about the matter. David and Mollie arranged with Sammy and Bertha to take them to Kilkeel to view the property a few days later. This was readily agreed, and that would give them a few days to give some thought to the proposal.

A few days later the two couples travelled over the Mourne Mountains to visit Seaview as they had previously arranged. The McNallys were not only impressed by what they saw, but they were also convinced that this was of the Lord and they readily agreed to give themselves whole-heartedly to this new venture and a new chapter in their lives.

As they travelled back to Lurgan David had a great sense of contentment and joy that Sammy and Bertha had agreed to take on this responsibility. Perhaps it was this joy that distracted him a little when his car hit a sheep that had strayed into the middle of the road. Sammy jokingly spoke up and said, "David, we should pick it up and put it in the freezer for the meals at Seaview."

Mervyn and Frances Moffett were CEF Directors for the Mourne area from 1968 to 1988 and were greatly blessed with thirty-five Good News Clubs in the area. For several years CEF had been endeavouring to find a suitable campsite for the Mission. In 1969 the CEF workers, Kenneth Martin, John and Irene Barfoot and Mervyn and Frances Moffett had organised the first CEF camp in Ireland with approximately forty campers with a team of helpers from across Northern Ireland at the Mourne Grange Private School on the Cranfield Road, Kilkeel.

The camp was such a success, and the school with its small church-like building seemed so suitable but they learned from the headmaster that the Mourne Grange Private School was not for sale.

Meanwhile, Mrs Mildred Haugh, who lived next door to the Seaview property in Kilkeel, contacted Mervyn and informed him that her neighbours, Mr and Mrs Harris, had decided to sell their bed and breakfast business. CEF had already had several camps at Seaview during the recent years, so Mervyn approached Mr and Mrs Harris about the possibility of them selling Seaview.

Mrs Harris affirmed that they were ready to sell their property and would like CEF to be able to buy it. The members of the CEF National Committee were overjoyed with this news. They knew that this was a big decision for them, a large step of faith. Because they were convinced that God was in this, they resolved decided not to haggle with Mrs Harris over the asking price; instead they would trust God to supply the money needed.

When a local estate agent heard that Seaview property was to be sold to CEF, he went to Mr and Mrs Harris and told them that he could put their house and business on the market and guaranteed that he could get them a far higher price. To this Mrs Harris replied, "No, I have promised it to CEF for the Lord's work among boys and girls, and I am not going back on my word."

John Barfoot was asked to make a slide presentation of the camp ministry and the need for CEF to purchase their own property. The Christian public responded admirably to this. As news about CEF acquiring the Kilkeel property funds came in quickly and this allowed them to purchase Seaview. Mr and Mrs Harris gladly sold the house with most of its contents to the CEF.

That was a big step, but it was only the first step. A lot of work needed to be done to transform and make the house suitable for the CEF camps.

Sammy and Bertha soon moved from their beloved Lurgan to Kilkeel and took up residence in the beautiful Kingdom of Mourne, undoubtedly an area of outstanding beauty. Robert Porter from Banbridge, another good friend of CEF and Mervyn and Frances Moffett, used his furniture van to move their belongings. Among the belongings, they took with them, was their beautiful organ that had been a gift from Mrs Best of the Christian bookshop.

After the van was loaded, Sammy led his helpers in a prayer of thanksgiving to God for how He had blessed Sammy and Bertha in their Hill Street home. Sammy also committed their future to the Lord as they embarked on this new CEF venture.

Just about the time Sammy and Bertha were due to move to Kilkeel a vesting order was made on their Hill Street home in Lurgan by the Northern Ireland Housing Executive. Their row of terrace houses was to be demolished to make way for new homes. Some neighbours had disputed with the Housing Executive officials about the price they were being offered for their homes. Sammy and Bertha knew they were leaving home to go to serve God in Kilkeel and therefore, they covenanted before God that they would accept whatever price was offered to them without dispute.

When the official arrived at their house, he explained to them why the house was being requisitioned and then told them how much was being offered for the small property. After Sammy and Bertha readily agreed with the sum offered the official said that within a few weeks they would receive a cheque in the post for the approved price, which Sammy understood to be several hundred pounds.

Some weeks later the cheque did arrive and instead of being several hundred pounds, much to their delight, it was several thousand pounds – ten times more than what they had expected.

Sammy and Bertha proved that God honours those who honour Him.

CHAPTER 8

# Moving In and Moving On

Moving from one property to another involves clearing out what is not needed and bringing in the new furnishings. Before the McNallys and friends could embark on the needed renovations at Seaview a lot of unwanted furniture and furnishings had to be cleared out. Old chairs were smelling of cigarette smoke, threadbare mats, and carpets, multiple books, and magazines were either carried to the local dump or burned.

Besides Sammy and Bertha working round the clock at the property, many friends volunteered their time and skills to help in the work. Joe Russell from the Portadown construction company, Russell Brothers, was a good friend and supporter of CEF. He sent workmen to do essential plumbing and electric work. Sammy's life-long friend from the Band Room in Lurgan, Jimmy Walker, returned day after day and was willing to do anything and everything that was needed. Alan Little of Little's Electrics, another close associate of Sammy and Bertha in Lurgan, helped take care of all the rewiring and electrical installations in the property. Willie McCullough, a nephew of the previous owner, Mrs Harris, installed a large modern kitchen for Bertha and her helpers to do the cooking.

One of the encouraging aspects of the preparatory work for CEF was to see the local response from Christians from all the local evangelical denominations. They rallied round to welcome CEF to the town and freely offered their help in many ways. Besides this, Christian friends and some non-Christians, from all over Northern Ireland freely offered to help CEF in this new venture for the Kingdom of God.

David McQuilken mobilised all the CEF fulltime workers to play their part in cleaning, washing, stripping walls, papering walls and painting window and doorframes. Mervyn Moffett, Kenneth Martin, John Barfoot and Henry Berry were only a few of those young men who worked ceaselessly at the property. The CEF lady workers also played their vital part in helping transform Seaview and make it habitable and comfortable for the children. Members of the CEF Mourne Committee toiled steadily to help in many practical ways to prepare the house for the first camp at Seaview in July 1975.

Sammy's former employer in Lurgan, Fred Wilson, provided a large roll of fabric for curtains. When it arrived, Bertha was hesitant to cut the material. Nell Gibson who lived locally was a skilled and professional seamstress who provided furnishings for some of Ulster's leading furniture shops. Nell, helped by Mabel Christie, soon got to work transforming the roll of material into curtains to provide lovely new drapes for all the windows in Seaview.

After clearing, cleaning, papering and painting the multiple bedrooms Sammy was not happy with so many double beds on the premises. They were fine for a bed and breakfast business but not suitable for a children's camp.

Sammy organised for these to be replaced with more serviceable bunk beds, which would increase the accommodation for the camps.

David McQuilken was noted for being very frugal and totally accountable in all his work. When the bunk beds arrived, he did not feel free to dispose of the old bedding as he thought they might come in handy some time. He asked Mervyn Moffett if he could borrow a van to transport the old iron framed bedding and mattresses to the third floor of the CEF office in Victoria Street in the centre of Belfast.

Mervyn borrowed a furniture van from Robert Porter in Banbridge. Sammy helped Mervyn and John Barfoot load all the iron frames and mattresses into the van until it was so tightly packed there was not room for anything. From Kilkeel, Mervyn and John travelled over to Banbridge to pick up Mervyn's wife, Frances, to accompany them to Belfast. All three clambered into the front seat of the van and were accompanied by the Moffett's little Jack Russell pet dog.

In 1975 Ulster's infamous "troubles" were at their height and there were army security checks all over the Province. On their way to Belfast, the CEF workers were inevitably stopped by the army at Sprucefield, near Lisburn. They were requested to open the back of the van. When the soldiers saw that the vehicle was packed to the roof, they told Mervyn that they would have to follow an army escort to Long Kesh where the van's contents would have to be unloaded, and the van inspected.

On arrival there, Mervyn and John were directed to a waiting room while Frances and the dog were taken to a very comfortable office. The security men were taken with the dog and after a short while brought it a big juicy steak to eat. The pet received better hospitality than Frances and the men.

While they waited soldiers unpacked the van and piled the metal beds and mattresses on the ground. After inspection, they were satisfied that the van was not a security risk, so they began to load the beds back into the vehicle. After the soldiers had piled the beds to the roof of the van they still had several beds over. John and Mervyn were called to help the soldiers load all the cargo.

All this took a lot of time, and it was well after 11.00 p.m. before the CEF removal team, and the dog was released to continue the trip to Belfast. It was almost midnight before they got to Victoria Street by which time they had resolved there was no way they were going to carry the beds to the third floor. They opened up the office, put the lights on and started to unload the contents of the van.

Within a short while, the police arrived and wanted to know what they were doing opening up the building at midnight and carrying bed frames into an office. Mervyn had to give them a convincing answer for the CEF office was adjacent to the Musgrave Street Police Station. The police officers were as amused as Mervyn and John and let them finish their chore.

It had been a long and very eventful day. All three CEF workers slept well that night, and there were no complaints from the dog.

The bed frames and mattresses were taken to the third floor the next morning and stored as David had requested. They remained there until CEF vacated the premises when they were finally dumped as scrap.

CHAPTER 9

# A Glorious Day

After weeks of frenzied work, the hustle and bustle, sweat and maybe a few tears, the Child Evangelism Fellowship's Camp and Conference Centre in Kilkeel was ready to be opened.

On a beautiful morning in June 1975, CEF workers and friends from all over Northern Ireland and beyond gathered on the driveway and lawns outside Seaview. Leslie McConnell provided a lorry from the quarry to be used as a platform for this Opening and Thanksgiving Service.

The Rev. David McGuaghey, minister of the local Mourne Presbyterian Church, led the proceedings and called on Molly McQuilken to cut the ribbon at the main entrance to the house. After this, eight-year-old Margaret Murphy, daughter of Mr Sam Murphy, a member of the CEF Mourne Committee, presented Molly with a bouquet of flowers. This was greeted with a great round of applause.

David McQuilken gave glory to God for His goodness and faithfulness in a marvellous testimony about how the conference centre had come into the hands of CEF. Fred Orr, a missionary to Brazil with Acre Gospel Mission, who had a close association with CEF in Ireland, gave the closing message. It was Fred who had led Sam Doherty to the Lord years earlier and had subsequently introduced Sam and Sadie to CEF.

Mildred Haugh, who lived next door to Seaview, had been the first person to indicate to CEF that Seaview was for sale. On the day of the opening, she and her family were not able to attend the opening service because her daughter Sharon had chickenpox. However, Mother and daughter had a great view of the proceedings from a safe distance at their upstairs window.

After the service, the grass lawns were covered with people sitting and chatting excitedly after their "grand tour" of the newly refurbished conference house. Sammy and Bertha were introduced to so many people that day. Although they were not able to retain all the names they were much encouraged to see how great a network of friends, supporters, and leaders of Good News Clubs stood behind the CEF work.

The day of celebration and thanksgiving was crowned by an abundance of refreshments at the local high school. CEF workers from all the areas in Northern Ireland had combined to provide this special meal.

Bertha and Sammy met Madge and Bobby Graham for the first time on the day of the opening. That encounter forged a lasting friendship. Madge, who had worked alongside George McCullough to start a GNC at Binnian Hall, became such a close friend to Bertha that when friends spoke of Madge, Bertha promptly "Oh, she's family to us."

After the McNallys retired Bobby and Madge entertained Sammy and Bertha for lunch every Sunday. When Madge and Bobby were invited out for Sunday lunch by other friends, Madge always made sure that Sammy and Bertha accompanied them and there was a place at the table for them also. That arrangement continued until Sammy went to be with the Lord, and then Madge and Bobby continued to have Bertha as their special guest for Sunday dinner.

After the large crowd of friends had drifted away, Sammy and Bertha's priority was to prepare for the upcoming camps in July. Instead of the annual two-week camp, they could organise weekly camps for different age groups during July and August. The maximum number at all previous CEF camps had been forty campers. With the increased capacity at Seaview, they now had accommodation for seventy children and staff.

Sammy transformed the front lawn into a pitch and putting green for the children. This was a great success and gave hours of fun to the campers for several years, however, after that they had to tear up the lawn and replace it with a car park. Previously visitors were parking their cars on the Harbour Road and caused some congestion and inconvenience, which did not lend to good neighbourliness.

Right from the beginning the Haugh family next door to Seaview were always good neighbours to Sammy and Bertha. It was not uncommon for Mildred to find that a cherry pie had been left on her doorstep, courtesy of Sammy and Bertha. These kindnesses were frequently reciprocated.

One day Sammy asked to borrow something from Mildred Haugh. Although Mildred's daughter, Sharon, was a very shy seven-year-old, Sammy, always quick to disarm nervous children, invited her to attend their Good News Club. That early introduction led to years of Sharon's involvement with her next-door neighbours. At first, she was withdrawn when new campers arrived, but soon she began to gain confidence. Before long she came out of her shell and was a willing helper each summer and at the Good News Club. Sammy and Mervyn Moffett encouraged Sharon so that her increased confidence led to increased participation. She gave out the chorus books at the meetings, played the piano, taught the memory verses, led the quiz time and also taught the Bible lessons.

Patricia Wilson, a former Faith Mission pilgrim, had time to spare before going to Switzerland for her term at the CEF Training Institute. Besides enjoying her time in the kitchen, Patricia met Jonathan Reid, a young man of many talents. Patricia was quiet and reserved, but Jonathan was outgoing and never lost for words. After Patricia and Jonathan were married, they returned to the Mourne area to work alongside Mervyn and Frances for their CEF field training.

In 1980 a sixteen-year-old girl, Sandra Shields, was invited by Sammy and Bertha to become their helper at Seaview. The Mission soon approved of Sandra joining the McNallys for the work. Bertha trained Sandra to do every job necessary in discharging their caretaking work at Seaview. Her first task was to iron 142 tea towels; each one featured a different place. Over the next years, she never backed down from any work that needed to be done. Bertha's missionary experience had taught her how to make a little go a long, long way. She tried to impart some of her wisdom and the lessons she had learned over the years to Sandra. At the annual autumn fair in Kilkeel, Bertha and Sandra bought lots of boxes of cooking apples.

They then spent a long time peeling, stewing them before storing the stewed apples in the freezer to be used for puddings and desserts during the summer camps.

Sandra worked tirelessly as an assistant to Bertha and Sammy, always painting, papering, revamping dull bedrooms, organising linen for beds, helping in the kitchen and looking after the general upkeep of the house.

Bertha and Sandra worked well together seeing to the daily routines of cleaning toilets and emptying bins, the weekly chores of mopping floors with buckets of water and bleach and then cleaning windows every month, Bertha doing the inside of the windows and Sandra doing the outside. Added to this the washing machine was in constant use and then the two ladies hung the washing on the clothes' lines to catch the fresh breezes coming from the Irish Sea. All the washing had to be ironed. When the two months of summer camps ended the whole house had to have "big clean" which included the washing of eighty woollen blankets.

Sammy also played a big part in all these chores although his main emphasis was the maintenance of the property. There was always plenty to do; repairing broken furniture or appliances, servicing the boilers and the electrics of the property and attending to the shrubs and lawns. Sammy also tried to develop more amenities for the children such as the football area and the games hut where the sports equipment was stored.

It seemed there was no end to the work at the Seaview Conference Centre. However, Sammy, Bertha, and Sandra were equal to the job.

Sandra worked with Sammy and Bertha for two years before they retired and were replaced by Dessie and

Margaret Wright. Sandra then stayed on for another five years during which time she made new curtains for all the windows on her little sewing machine as well as seeing to a hundred and one other little jobs to keep Seaview running efficiently. She also continued leading the Good News Club at Seaview. This was a great training ground for Sandra to develop her teaching skills. The children and adults loved her quick wit and pleasant presentations.

When Sandra announced she was leaving Seaview to go to Bible College in England the news was greeted with a mixture of sadness and joy.

The permanent staff at Seaview were greatly helped and encouraged by many volunteers who arrived to freely assist the team. Bertha's close friend, Amy McBurney, who had spent twenty-eight years as a missionary in Nepal and India, had arrived home to Kilkeel to care for her aged mother. Amy volunteered to go Seaview every Monday to help Bertha with the washing and ironing of the previous week's bedding. Bertha reciprocated Amy's gesture by attending a missionary prayer meeting at Amy's home every Wednesday evening. They had a special friendship.

Sammy and Bertha recognised that all the activity would be in vain without God's blessing on the overall work. Although they did everything to make the centre comfortable and suitable for the children, their greatest burden was to see boys and girls come to know Christ as Saviour.

Not long after Sandra arrived at Seaview, she could hear Sammy walking up and down the lounge upstairs making lots of mumbled noises. She was a little bit puzzled and concerned, so she asked Bertha, "What is Sammy doing up there?"

Bertha explained, "He is not talking to himself. He is talking to the Lord and praying out loud for the campers and the children of the Good News Club."

Sammy McNally was a very practical person and also a great man of prayer.

CHAPTER 10

# Camp

A week at the Seaview camp was an event that hundreds of boys and girls looked forward to every year. For many, it was the highlight of the year, and for some the only holiday they would have. When the camp was in full swing during July and August about sixty children arrived each week. That meant that effective Bible teaching was given to more than six hundred children every summer.

Months before the camp lots of preparation had to be carried out by the area directors. Those who attended the Good News Clubs got priority in their applications for places at camp. The area director was responsible for appointing counsellors for their group and had to process the applications. Since those early days, the campers were limited to children between ages of nine to fourteen. Youth groups would be developed later with the emergence of CEF's Youth Challenge.

Buses, mini buses, and cars transported excited children on Saturday afternoons from all over the country to Kilkeel. Maybe not all of the children were excited. For some, it might have been there first time away from home and were a little intimidated by meeting other children they did not know or sleeping in a dormitory with several other kids.

Sammy and Bertha were always there to welcome each group to Seaview and try to put the campers at ease. Very soon everyone, young and old, was speaking of "Uncle Sammy and Auntie Bertha." After the first meal provided by Auntie Bertha, Sammy took a few moments to speak to all the campers about the "Seaview rules" for the week. Basically, it was about respecting and protecting the property without spoiling the children's fun. Although Sammy was kind and highly respected, he did not tolerate any nonsense or bad behaviour.

After that introduction, Sammy and Bertha played a background role for the rest of the week and allowed the camp leaders to get on with their programme. They were only called on when something broke down, or an emergency arose.

Although there were eight different camp groups each summer led by the respective area director and a team of helpers and counsellors, the programme for the week followed a similar pattern. After their first meal on arrival and Sammy's introductory talk, the camp director told the children about the hours for the "tuck shop" and how they could deposit their money in the "camp bank."

Each day began with the "dorm quiet time" when the dorm leader would read and pray with the campers. After breakfast, the campers had to return to tidy their rooms and do some chores.

The campers were split into two groups, one to learn a missionary story and the other to engage in handcrafts. In mid-morning, after a short break, the two groups switched over for the same classes.

Bertha always had a sumptuous meal ready for the children who lined up to be served at the hatch in the dining room. The counsellors were designated to teams to have their day to help in the "wash up" after the meals. After lunch the "camp bank" and "tuck shop" were opened for business.

In the afternoon's various activities were planned for the children; a day at the beach, sports day, a bus outing to Tollymore or Castlewellan Forest Park, a visit to the shops or a "find the worker day." These were always exciting and memorable times.

The "hunt the worker," which generally took place on Friday afternoons was one of the campers' favourite events. On that afternoon the staff and workers had to leave the camp, disguise themselves and remain visible in a public place in the town without hiding. Thirty minutes later the campers were sent out to try to find them. The workers came up with many ingenious ways to fool the children.

One worker took a pair of garden hedge clippers and in the town acted as though he was a council worker snipping at the grass on a public lawn. While unsuspectingly working and clipping at the grass a man approached him and said, "What are you doing? We have men who cut this grass with machines every week." Although a little embarrassed, the CEF worker explained why he was disguising himself as a council worker, much to the amusement of the council officer.

At another "hunt, the worker" search a leader had a different bright idea. He dressed up in his best suit and went down to a clothing shop in the town. In the shop window, there were several tailors' dummies dressed in suits and other clothing that was advertised for sale. The CEF worker told the shop owner who he was and explained about the camp and their Friday game. He said the children would soon be looking for him and asked if he could take up a position in the shop window disguised as a tailor's dummy. Although the owner laughed at the idea, he happily agreed to cooperate. The CEF worker climbed into the shop window, took a position beside the other dummies and stood motionless. He looked just one of the shop's models.

On that day the campers found all the workers except this one. The disguised "CEF dummy" could see the children searching up and down the street and frequently passing the shop window. They never thought of looking at the shop window.

However, the "CEF dummy" also noticed a young couple walking along the street hand in hand, obviously revealing that they were very much in love. As they walked, they were looking in various shop windows, probably making decisions about what furniture they should buy for their new home.

They finally stopped in front of the window where the "CEF dummy" was standing. They looked at all the dummies in the window without any suspicions. Just when the young man turned to look away at something else, the young lady looked straight at the "CEF dummy." He could not resist the temptation to wink at her. She was startled. She looked again, and the "dummy" repeated the wink. The girl turned to her fiancé and told him what she'd seen. He looked at the "CEF dummy," which had returned to its stiff stance as if it was frozen to the spot.

The two sweethearts began to argue. She insisted the dummy had winked at her and he said she had imagined things. They walked away still arguing. The CEF worker hoped he had not upset their wedding plans, but he was soon on his way back to Seaview to tell the campers where he had been.

Every evening the general meeting was for everyone. At it, a Bible lesson, the memory verses were taught, and Bible quizzes were enjoyed. The workers hoped that at the end of a full day the children would be exhausted and ready for a good night's sleep. However, young people are bundles of energy, and it seemed that they found added verve to stay awake until the wee hours of the morning – much to the annoyance of the leaders.

Besides the camps during July and August and the workers' training weeks in June, various church groups used the Seaview Conference Centre during most weekends throughout the year. Outside of the camp season, ministerial groups used the premises for their annual prayer retreats or fellowship conferences.

The purchase of Seaview was a wise and timely investment for eternity.

# CHAPTER 11

# Here and There

After the camp season finished Sammy and Bertha packed into their caravan all they needed for their own vacation. They took young Sandra Shields with them for she had become like a daughter to them. Some folks referred to Sandra as the "little McNally girl."

The threesome set off to travel all over the countryside, mostly in the South of Ireland. They covered hundreds of miles visiting churches and Christian friends in many places. Sammy made sure he was well supplied with plenty of tracts for distribution wherever they went. They loved to call with John and Joan Nixon, CEF workers engaged in a unique caravan ministry in the city of Cork. By the end of September, these well-travelled workers returned to Seaview to pick up the reins of another busy season at the Seaview Conference Centre.

Back in Lurgan Sammy's sisters who still lived in Hill Street were ill and needed personal attention as they neared the end of life's journey. Bertha frequently travelled to Lurgan to care for them and look after them during their final days. While Bertha was caring for Sammy's sisters in Lurgan Charlie and Cynthia Shields, Sandra's parents, invited Sammy for dinner every evening. Much to

Cynthia's delight, Sammy wrote in her visitors' book, "Great soup served here."

During Bertha's prolonged absence Sandra Shields had to take on extra responsibilities. When she got frustrated, she always had her mother to fall back on. One morning she phoned her mother and asked, "How do you cook seventy-eight eggs for breakfast?" Cynthia soon arrived at Seaview to help her distressed daughter provide enough hot food for the hungry campers.

After Sandra left for Bible School in England, she was much missed. It was just at that time that the Lord called another young lady to take Sandra's place in Seaview. Valerie Swanson, who hailed from Moneymore, was small in stature but had a broad smile and a big heart. Valerie quickly fitted into the team. Like Sandra, Valerie was a hard worker who was loved by everyone. Also, as Sandra before her, after a few years at Seaview, Valerie left for Bible School and then to the CEF work in Sligo.

In all the coming and goings at the Seaview Conference centre, Sammy and Bertha were constant, overseeing the kitchen, caring for the property and organising for camps and groups. However, after seven years at Seaview, they felt it was time for them to retire.

The 24th May 1982 was a day of mixed feelings. It was Sammy and Bertha's final day of service at Seaview. To mark the occasion, unknown to the McNallys, their CEF colleagues had planned a surprise meal at High Street Presbyterian Church hall. Kenny and Mary Martin had arranged to take the retiring couple on an outing that would pass through Lurgan, their hometown. On arrival there Kenny casually suggested they go into the High Street

Church hall since the door seemed to be open. When Sammy and Bertha entered the church hall they were shocked to be welcomed by a round of applause from all their CEF colleagues. They were invited to be guests of honour for a lovely meal that had been prepared by the CEF workers.

There was plenty of chatter and laughter around the tables as everyone had a story to tell about the well-known and highly respected hosts at Seaview. As the meal was drawing to a close, Kenny Martin stepped up to where Sammy and Bertha were sitting. With a big red book in his hand he loudly announced, "Sammy and Bertha McNally, this is your life."

Kenny conducted the couple into the main church hall where up to three hundred friends had gathered to enjoy an evening of fun and fellowship as Kenny Martin reviewed the wonderful lives of this unique couple. He and others spoke highly of the McNally's seven years at Seaview and how they had catered for the physical and spiritual welfare of thousands of children. Young people, co-workers and friends testified of the influence and blessing Sammy and Bertha had been on their lives. It was a memorable evening.

A generous retirement gift given to them at the end of the evening enabled Sammy and Bertha to visit family, colleagues, and friends in Canada, Africa, New Zealand, and India. Since her days in India Bertha had kept in touch with her friends around the world.

With their retirement from Seaview Bertha and Sammy needed a home of their own. They discovered a suitable but small house in Meeting House Lane in Kilkeel. The house named, "Sandy Row," needed some renovations, so Sammy called again on his friends to help. Soon they got to work refurbishing the house and developing a bonus room upstairs for overnight guests. Bertha called this "the prophet's chamber."

Sammy's friend from Portadown, Joe Russell, who had helped in the refurbishment of Seaview, stood by Sammy again to help in the renovations to their new home. Alan Little and Jimmy Walker travelled from Lurgan to see to the electrics and other adjustments to the property. Sandra's dad, Charlie Shields, built a beautiful stone fireplace for the house. Added to these many local friends were on hand to help with painting and decorating the McNallys new abode.

Throughout their years in Kilkeel Sammy and Bertha worshipped at Kilkeel Presbyterian Church, which is adjacent to Meetinghouse Lane. They were surrounded by their many good friends in the town lacked for nothing. Either they were being invited for meals by various families, or food was delivered to their home by some of the fine local cooks.

They maintained their interest and involvement in the Seaview Conference Centre and even after their retirement Sammy and Bertha gave up their home to accommodate the occasional overflow at Seaview. When this happened Sammy and Bertha went to stay at the home of their good friends Mr & Mrs Patton.

Sammy and Bertha enjoyed their cosy home in "Meeting House Lane" until the Lord called Sammy to a better home in heaven in 2004. During the early days of his terminal illness Bertha nursed and cared for Sammy at home, but eventually, he had to go into Brooklands Nursing Home. While he was there the McNallys' faithful friends, Mrs Patton, Bobby and Madge Graham and others took Bertha to visit Sammy.

It was after thirty-six years of a happy and devoted marriage union that Sammy and Bertha were parted when Sammy passed into the presence of his Lord. He was 91 and Bertha was 86.

Although Bertha missed Sammy, the Lord upheld and strengthened her in her sorrow. Initially, she was able to stay in her little home and maintained the "open door" welcome to all visitors.

Finally, Bertha had to leave Meeting Street Lane on 31st August 2017, to become a resident at Slieve Roe House, Kilkeel. On her arrival, she quickly made new friends and entertained them by playing hymns on the piano or with her mouth organ.

While writing this book, Bertha often said to me (Christine Bell) that she felt that she had lived four different lives. I think she lived more than four lives for she has packed so much into her ninety-four years. This lady from Lurgan has faithfully served her Lord for eight decades, and perhaps that is the reason behind her constant smile and those twinkling and happy eyes.

Bertha lived simply and humbly, and it is her wish that she might die with the same dignity. She has been a special lady whose life has made a difference in those who have benefitted from knowing her. Today, many rise up to call her blessed for she has blessed multitudes of people all over our world.

# Postscript

As this book goes to press Bertha will soon celebrate her 95th birthday. To mark a previous birthday several years ago a good friend, Amy McBurney, organised a special "Bertha McNally This is Your Life" programme. Bobby and Madge Graham initially thought they could not be there for the special night so they sent a letter that surveyed Bertha's life. Their original plans changed allowing to be present for the celebration. Here is what they had written.

We are sure that as you pass another milestone in your life you can hardly believe the experiences you've had since you were a little girl in Lurgan. Being the youngest of four boys and three girls, you always appreciated your loving family. Sadly, you lost both your parents early in life. With the rest of the family, you decided to venture out into the wide, wide world. However, it would seem that even then a certain Mr McNally had already stirred your heart as you helped him with his children's meetings in the famous Band Room. Of course, you made sure your secret thoughts were hidden from him. Nevertheless, as time passed you went off to train as a nurse and midwife in England. You graduated in 1947 as SRN and SCM. In due course, you spent some time as a district nurse in Scotland where many were heartened by your loving Christian care and attention.

God's call on your life led you to India via Mount Hermon Missionary College in England where you trained for two years. Your fifteen years in India with your orphan boys and leprosy clinics hold many happy memories. Even yet you keep all correspondence with someone you knew then in different capacities. It would be good if you could write down some of the highlights of those years for us.

Again, the same Sammy McNally who had stirred your heart many years previously, wrote to you with a "proposition" – not the proposal, of marriage. Of course, you were on your own when you got this letter and so, as you had no one with whom to share the good news, you just cried. We know that these were tears of joy and soon you were on your way home to marry the man of your dreams in 1968.

For a few years your home was in Lurgan, but in the early 1970s, CEF decided to buy Seaview as an outreach centre for children and young people. They were looking for a couple to manage and lead this outreach and so the McNally's arrived in the Kingdom of Mourne.

The opening of Seaview in June 1975 was when the Graham family first met and formed a lasting friendship with Sammy and Bertha. All of our children grew up knowing you as uncle Sammy and auntie Bertha as if you were part of our family. They enjoyed your visits to our home at Silent Valley. Now we know how much you enjoy your visit to their homes.

You successfully set the pattern at Seaview for the years ahead. You both shared your love for children and young people by showing them the love of Jesus as you ministered to them and sought to draw them to our Saviour.

On retirement, you moved to your newly built home, Maranatha in Meetinghouse Lane. Still wanting to see more, you went for a few months tour around the world visiting your very old friends in India and family and friends in New Zealand and Canada. This time was thoroughly enjoyed as you visited and experienced so many things that most of us can only read about.

Back home you were off again in your little caravan, travelling around Ireland during several summers and continued to spread God's good news, encouraging believers and making many new friends in the towns and villages you visited.

Sammy was called home in September 2004. Bertha, you showered your love, care, and devotion on him.

From the seven members of your family, you are the only one left. You have nephews in Belfast and New Zealand, and I know you keep in touch with those who live so far away.

We all know how much you are appreciated and loved by people all around you and from within our church family. In the days that lie ahead, whatever God allows, we trust and pray that you will know His richest blessing, good health, and an abundance of good friends who love you so dearly.

God bless you, Bertha, we love you so much.

**Bobby and Madge (Graham)**